Becky....

THE BOOK OF WIMMIN

from

Diane
1986

The Book

OF

WIMMIN

An ANTHOLOGY *of* CONTEMPORARY FEMINISM

Compiled by

TWO MEN

*

With illustrations by MICHAEL HEATH ESQ.

PRIVATE EYE

MCMLXXXVI

Published in Great Britain
1986

Private Eye Productions Limited
6 Carlisle Street, London W1
in association with André Deutsch Limited
105-106 Great Russell Street, London WC1

9 8 7 6 5 4 3 2

ISBN 233 97986 7

Printed in Great Britain by
Richard Clay (The Chaucer Press)
Bungay, Suffolk

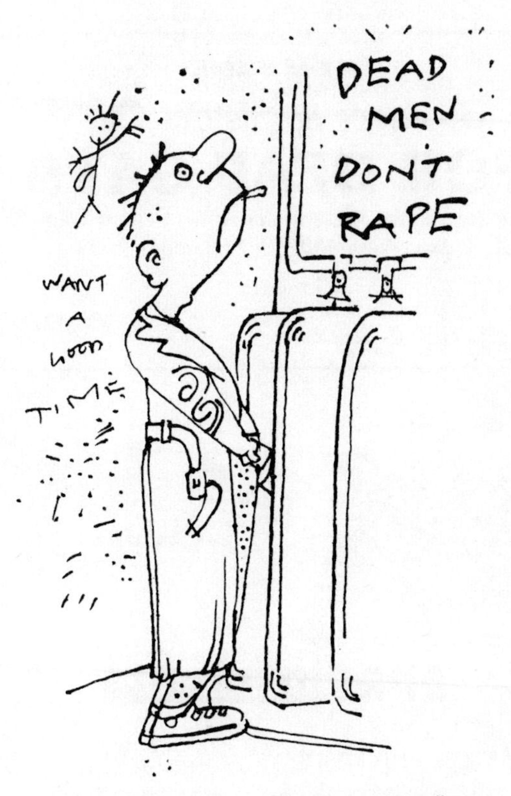

Graffiti, London toilet

announcements

FRIDAY 8 APRIL

Brothers & Sisters Club

FOR DEAF GAYS

meet upstairs at the Westminster Arms, Storeys Gate, SW1
(tubes: Westminster & St James's Park)

8 pm.

CAPITAL GAY

appointments

SERC/ASTON UNIVERSITY

C.R. WHEELER & PARTNERS

Teaching Company Associate

The post is equally open to men and women, but applications are particularly welcome froın women.

OPR Society Newsletter

art

Betty Kalache's work is a sculptural response to the significance of the sense of touch. On show are two sets of work, one set refers to the Velasquez painting 'The Toilet of Venus' and the other work to Poussin's 'Bacchanalian'.

The human body, the use of muslins, and motherhood are main considerations in the making of the works. These are produced by having direct contact with a living model who is draped in muslins saturated with plaster. These 'moulages' are hung on washing lines as a homage to all the women in human history that have spent years and years washing their hands and brains away during child bearing and rearing.

The Women Artists Slide Library
in Collaboration with the Gallery Co-ordinators
of Battersea Arts Centre

A second reading of the Pandora's Box Myth sees women as open to more levels of experience than men, who fear and trap it. Mouse Katz's soft sculptures shoot big pink penises at you with frantic ringing bells; show 'Venus Trapped Like a Fly' in green grasping leaf-hands stuck with pins or a terrified white man confronted by wild purple-haired Pandora.

SPARE RIB, Exhibition review

AFRICA CENTRE
38 King St., EC2 (836 1973) Covent Gdn tube.
Mon–Fri 9.30 am–5.30pm.

Veronica Ryan's wooden men stand, pricks extended and flowering into paintbrushes to parody the equation of genius with (masculine) sexual drive, or blossoming into a shower hose from which words pour out to pollute our minds. Torture, rape, oppression, famine, bitterness, despair – the fruits of phallic masculinity – stream over the rigid torso. In contrast a group of full, fecund shapes, represent the female principle. Pod, egg and bean shapes seem ready to burst into new life, but chances of survival seem slim, faced with the collective hysteria of male aggression.

Sarah Kent, TIME OUT

YOUNG WOMEN'S

POSTER DESIGN

COMPETITION

Young women under 21 are invited to design a poster depicting themselves and their lives in a 'non-stereotyped and positive way', in a competition being organised by the See Red Women's Workshop.

Entries are particularly welcome from young women who are Black, Jewish, Lesbian, have disabilities, are mothers, unemployed or live in Scotland, Ireland or Wales.

There will be no overall winner of the competition.

SCRAPSTORE Newsletter

Gone are the equipment, outfits and contortions of male-dominated pornography. Nancy's fantasies are acrobatic in a cerebral sense. They express an admixture of physical contentment and spiritual ecstasy. She sets her scenes in cosmic landscapes of glowing colour. Male genitalia, female breasts and buttocks (androgynous) are outlined as part of a generalised locale. But the crucial point is what is happening inside the woman's body and, by extension, in her mind.

Review of Nancy Kruseman
at the Stephen Bartley Gallery

SAT 4 TO FRI 23 JAN

FEMINIST BEERMATS

An exhibition by Jo Lurkesse and Eudoria Willmott

Commissions taken.
Rosehampton Library, Danebury Avenue, SW15.

WHAT'S ON in Wandsworth

books

To precis her views: we live in a cockocratic state. A sado-state. The planet is dominated by phallocracy. Men are rapists and women-batterers. Patriarchy is the source of all social evils. Nuclearism, chemical contamination of the earth, planned famine, torture of political prisoners, torture of laboratory animals, obscene medical experimentation, are all 'discharges of male instinctual energy through activities that are socially approved by males.' Among those singled out for castigation are God, Ronald Reagan, the Pope, Gandhi, T.E. and D.H. Lawrence, Dag Hammarskjöld, Robert Oppenheimer and Dustin Hoffman in 'Tootsie'.

CITY LIMITS review of
'Pure Lust' by Mary Daly

Parallels with the Christian and ancient Greek traditions give these enchanting myths an air of universality. Copper Woman, the symbolic matriarch of the Nootka, creates man from her own snot, and with him and the rulers of the heavens, sons and daughters are born to populate the four corners of the earth. The Old Woman's timeless wisdom and knowledge was thus passed on and preserved, the female influence remaining dominant throughout.

HILARY TAGG, review of
'Daughters of Copper Woman'
by Ann Cameron

Suniti Namjoshi will be reading from her new book

THE CONVERSATIONS OF COW (Women's Press, £2.95) at the Silver Moon Bookshop, 68 Charing Cross Road, London WC2, on 26 September at 6.30pm. Admission free, women only.

This sharply satirical book is built around the dialogue between lesbian separatist Suniti and Bhadravati a Brahmin lesbian cow, goddess of a thousand faces and a thousand manifestations. Witty and inventive it challenges our every assumption about how we relate to each other.

Press Release

The Daughters of Egalia

by Gerd Brantenberg

A complete reversal of sex-roles, down to the minutest detail.

Very funny and close to the bone. A book where men are called "housebounds", where they wear curlers in their beards and curtsey after a dance.

Read it, it's worth it!

OUTWRITE

The *Wanderground* by Sally Miller Gearhart, a don at San Francisco State University, is an altogether heavier tale of an age of male-dominated cities and wilderness-dwelling communes of free women who can fly and talk to the animals . . .

> "Suddenly a blaze of colour stunned her mind-stretch. Such force! She stopped, pulled in her spanners and her channel reach to Seja.". . .

There are future gays as well:

> "The Gentles. Men who knew that the outlaw women were the only hope for the earth's survival. Men, who, knowing that maleness touched women only with the accumulated hatred of centuries, touched no women at all."

SUNDAY TIMES MAGAZINE

Goodbye Sleeping Beauty
The Female Experience in Fairy Tales
by Madonna Kolbenschlag

In a subtle reassessment of popular fairy tales, the author shows that there is more to the female role than passivity, waiting for her knight in shining armour.

Sleeping Beauty . . . has a phoenix-like quality announcing an awakening and advance in spiritual maturity. Beauty . . . is our age's authentic heroine. A woman who is secure in her own identity achieves liberation personally and socially, and is able to help others, being feminist and feminine at the same time.

Marion Boyars, Book Catalogue 83/84

Louise Lacey – LUNACEPTION

This is an unusual story of the author's search for a new approach to contraception and the discoveries that search led to. After investigating all the generally used techniques she came upon the technique of 'lunaception', which could be used to determine when she would ovulate and also enabled her to synchronize her body cycle with the phases of the moon and thus make a connection between herself and the universe.

She tells how it helps her predict, for a given day, her mood, her energy level and even her self image – and she supplies charts and other information needed to try the technique.

Catalogue of YES!, Penguin Bookship

TALKING POINT

People just don't know how to write stories about women. People don't even know what women are now. They certainly don't know how to write about men and women together. So love stories have to be about extra-terrestrials or between two women or a man dressed as a woman.

Susan Sarandon, 'Dawn'

In the British Library Anna meets Karen, a teacher at the North London Poly, a "freelance socialist feminist intellectual" working on women and masochism. As Anna helps her with her flagellation studies, they fall in love;

Karen preaches that "the dyke is the positive image of the negative virgin". Anna finds Karen's lesbian friends congenial too – a "women's house" seems not unlike a convent.

A review of 'Virgin Territory' by Sarah Maitland

FEMINIST AUDIO BOOKS' subscription service is only available to blind or reading impaired women.

However, there is no way that we can prevent men, who may be living with these women, from listening to any tape. In addition, other people are planning to set up an 'alternative' socialist tape library for men and women. F.A.B. will be making arrangements to share some tapes with them. Blind women can then subscribe to both services.

We do appreciate, however, that there are women who would not want to put their energy into taping books which men may read. If you feel like this, *please discuss this when you ring up to select a book.*

Feminist Audio Books

'In *Ruth* I have spotlighted the woman we all fear to be, the sexually unattractive loser who is expected to opt out – instead she opts back in, joins the enemy and triumphs by behaving badly . . . it is not an anti-feminist book, it takes courage to burn down one's house and give away one's children – the feminist will certainly approve of that bit . . .'

Fay Weldon, TIME OUT

RED BEANS & RICE ($4.95, cloth $10.95) by Bode Noonan, *illustrated by Diana Souza* offers "recipes for lesbian health and wisdom", in the form of six essays by a New Orleans writer on lesbian life and dining in the U.S.

PUBLISHERS WEEKLY

children

Schoolboys are being encouraged to dress in girls' clothes in a scheme to eradicate sexism.

The boys, aged up to seven, dress in skirts and petticoats and carry handbags.

They also cook and play with dolls while girls play with engineering sets in the Inner London Education Authority's scheme to combat 'sexism and stereotyping'.

MAIL ON SUNDAY

Once upon a time toddlers would sing 'The farmer wants a wife . . .' and other well-loved rhymes.

Not any more, if the Women's Committee of the GLC has its way. The traditional words discriminate against gay men and lesbian women, says the committee.

The suggested 'non-heterosexist' version is 'The farmer wants a friend'.

Alternative games to 'Mummy and Daddy' should be found, it says. 'Tell children that many women live with other women, men with men, other adults, as well as alone, or with several in heterosexual couples.'

Anthony Duran, DAILY MAIL

. . . Take Jude's re-worked nursery rhymes.
This is her version of Humpty Dumpty:

Humpty Dumpty sat on a wall
Humpty Dumpty had a great fall
All the king's horses and all the king's men
couldn't put Humpty together again . . .
But his wife managed it in between
doing the washing, cooking, housework,
bringing up virtually single handed their
three yolks and appearing intermittently
at the local magistrates court charged
with shoplifting.

EXPRESS AND STAR

WARNING

Lavish affection on your child today and he could turn into an oppressor of your sex tomorrow.

THE GUARDIAN

Norah's Ark

Ann and Reg Cartwright

When the flood comes to Puddle Farm, capable Norah builds an ark for her animals and their adventures afloat begin. Stunning full-page pictures help make this a definite "must" for 4–7s. (32pp £3.50)

LETTERBOX LIBRARY

A small child has to find out all herm* can about the world and herm's own standing in it. The relationship of the adult world to children is more important, during the early years, than any question of gender or race.

**Herm = her/him, or she/he as applicable. Such a word is essential when considering child development (and at any other time too).*

LYSISTRATA MAGAZINE

TALKING POINT

Only women rear children, and in the pre-rational, animal-poetic stages of infancy act as first witness, boss, love, hate and other, which creates our split consciousness and deep human malaise. Basic gender divisions from the hidden foundations for female monogamy and male polygamy, engender male possessiveness and desire for control, force the mother-raised boy to project himself out on the world, and encourage female inferiority.

Nicci Garrard, MS PRINT

HE BEAR, SHE BEAR

Stan and Jan Berenstain

Cartoony pictures and jolly rhyming text make this an excellent book for the very young and beginner readers. Pictures of male bears knitting and females driving cranes illustrate the message: "We can do all these things you see, whether we are he OR she". (48pp £2.00)

LETTERBOX LIBRARY

courses

STUDY GROUP CLASSES

Vomiting as weight control

Classes start on Friday October 12th at 8pm.
10 sessions for £25

at 41, Kitchener Road, Portswood, Southampton.
For further details phone Carol Waskett on S. 554824.

DUE SOUTH MAGAZINE

BOOKWRITING WORKSHOP
To write, illustrate and self-produce books for children in a lesbian community. Thursdays 7.30 to 10.30 for ten weeks, starting 15th September. Phone the office for more details.

Dalston Children's Centre Programme

Christina Artemis, who describes herself as a High Priestess of Life, is holding a training session billed to "discover the Goddess within you".

The unique course offers women everywhere the chance to discover their "feminine power and divinity". Goddess training aims to teach women to discover their own beauty, personal magic and sexuality.

On top of that you can expect to experience two rebirths during the training weekends.

Richmond and Twickenham Times

International Summer Courses
AT THE DANISH FEMINIST SCHOOL

AUGUST 5–18

Reclaim the Power of Menstruation

AUGUST 19 – SEPTEMBER 1

Our Daily Peace

For further details write to:
Kvindehøjskolen, Visby, 6270 Tønder, Denmark.

Green, CND Newsletter

HAVE YOU EVER WANTED TO TRY OPERATING A FORK LIFT TRUCK?

If you are a woman, here is your chance.
To mark International Women's Day on March 8
The GLC is organising a week of events which include the opportunity to use heavy machinery at open days for women at GLC refuse depots.

THE LONDONER

The ovular series continues, on Thursdays, in the Western Common Room at 1 pm. (We've called them 'ovulars' in contrast to the male word 'seminar' – seminal implies the last word, the experts talking. 'Ovular', we believe, has connotations of growing, developing ideas together, not as experts but as equals. When we first used the word a lot of people, especially men, said it was silly or offensive, or both . . .)

The Thursday Women, University of New England

WOMEN'S EDUCATION GROUP MEETING

Anti-sexist and anti-racist approach to teaching acids and bases. All women science teachers welcome to attend. Thursday 30 January, 5pm, at Women's Education Centre, ILEA Drama and Tape Centre, Princeton Street, WC1.

CONTACT, ILEA magazine

Sign in York Bakers

LESBIAN FEMINIST WRITERS CONFERENCE

To be held on Sunday 5th February from 10 a.m. at the Hampden Community Centre, 150 Ossulston Street, London NW1.

Topics will include lesbian herstory, humour, political writing, poetry, academic writing, journalism, form, theatre, novel, accessibility.

WIPLASH – Women In Publishing

We now allow men to attend our seminars, but we do not allow them to ask questions. This seems to be a sensible solution because however well-meaning or feminist a man may be, he is still sexist because he is a man.

Letter to TIMES
EDUCATIONAL SUPPLEMENT

cinema

Re: "Feminist Strategies", May 1984.

Robin Wood's review of the film *Born in Flames* comes close to the absolutely fundamental issue in women's "struggle against male oppression" but does not quite hit the mark. Wood indicates a clear preference for *Born in Flames* which is "uncompromising in its call to militancy, revolution, and the overthrow of the symbolic phallus, represented by the radio tower blown up at the end."

Margaret Frenette, CANADIAN FORUM

CLOTHESLINES is an amusing and poetic documentary which focuses on laundry as an aspect of women's lives and work in the home. It is composed largely of tales and memories, both humorous and provocative.

The film touches on such themes as: the clothesline as a form of communication and measurement of a woman's success; a sense of order and arrangement as it reflects aesthetics; standards of whiteness; the sensory pleasures of handling fabric; men's place in these activities; perception of cleanliness and feelings of connection with other women, including inter-generational links.

South Australian Institute of Teachers Newsletter

IMAGES OF OURSELVES
A Women Only Event

Size Ten & Near the Big Chakra

are two films which offer an alternative view of women to those presented to us by the media. SIZE TEN focuses on three women of different sizes and ages. NEAR THE BIG CHAKRA shows an alternative to pornographic views of the vaginal area.

A discussion on both films will follow during which we hope to construct a new unencumbered image of ourselves. Please bring any pictures of yourself and/or magazine clips.

Malvern Festival Fringe Programme

Judith Higginbottom in her films depicts menstrual and moon images through her dreamwork. The effect is a beautiful addition to our modern lives from our mythological past. Her work includes "Water into Wine", a menstrual film; "Remember Me" and "Mysteries" about research through history/herstory using suffragette images; "Well Below", about Celtic women and the well, the water of life. She is currently working on an extension of "Water into Wine" called "Red Running Woman".

FEMINIST ACTION

Of all the silent comedians Laurel and Hardy are perhaps the most threatening to women, as they combine the physical ruination with misogyny. One epicene and gross, the other emaciated. They are an aesthetic offence, with their disaster-prone bodies and their exclusive relationship that not only shuts out women but questions their very necessity. They constitute a two man wrecking team of female – that is civilised and bourgeois – society.

Molly Haskell, 'From Reverence to Rape'

According to this view, the traditional cinematic "gaze" – the camera's point of view – is male. The male subject is constituted as voyeur and the woman is constituted as the object viewed. All cinematic pleasure is therefore male. Beginnings, middles and ends are male; climaxes are male; conflict is male; the usual styles and pace of editing are male; and so on. The camera is a phallus (read the literature of Women Against Pornography for the literalization of this notion that the camera is an organ of penetration), and women get fucked (over) by it.

LOS ANGELES WEEKLY

An accessible movie which, unusually, hinges not just on a woman but on a working-class Cuban woman who, not so unusually, is a wife, a mother and a breadwinner. When I saw it the reels were shown in the wrong order, but it seemed to make a lot of sense. Perhaps that's because women's roles are designed to cope with all eventualities.

Helen Mackintosh, CITY LIMITS

The best in new video plays in the tiny, rickety screening room of Cinema Parallele, farther south on The Main. *Here in the Southwest* shows a group of lesbians living in the American southwest with their castrated cat. Among other things, they talk rather wistfully about a certain kind of lizard that has only one sex – female – and which reproduces itself parthenogenetically (without fertilization). Later in the video, the women, equipped with butterfly nets and photocopies of a picture of said saurian, go out lizard-hunting but to no avail.

GLOBE & MAIL MONTREAL

A QUESTION OF SILENCE

A new and highly provocative narrative fiction film which analyses women's oppression. United in an unspoken bond in defense of a woman apprehended by a male boutique owner for shoplifting, two women join with her in mutilating and beating him to death. The repressive ideology of the patriarchal legal system which brings them to trial is challenged in the ensuing drama, as a female psychiatrist, who has previously prided herself on "making it" in a man's world, prepares a report on their sanity: taking a sex-less stand on such an issue is impossible, she can no longer subsume her femaleness. Often highly amusing (for women) and pulling no punches in relation to men, the film manages to integrate substantial analysis into a fictional format without making the tail wag the dog. An extraordinary first feature from writer/director Marleen Gorris. Dutch dialogue with subtitles.

Tyneside Cinema Handout

drama

Tonight at 8 o'clock is the last chance to see Jack Sanger's new play *The Rebuild* at the Kenny Theatre in the University Village at UEA.

The play concerns the arguments and meditations of three women as they strip down a car engine and simultaneously build up a life together without the need for what they each, in their different ways, think of as dishonest, manipulative men.

EASTERN DAILY PRESS

Interspersed in the plot are short sketches where woman – a grotesque caricature with balls of wool for her hair and a plastic laundry basket for a skirt – leaps around to bongo drums conquering nuclear waste, macho men and exploitation of women. Men are portrayed as being cold, insensitive and arrogant by the use of masks, maybe not an original idea but still an effective one.

Paola Tich, THE MANCUNION

We last met the Four Marys – and their secret gang dedicated to liberty, equality, sorority and solving jolly intriguing mysteries – battling against the nuclear threat. We re-join our chums from 4b as they enter the Fifth Form and their final year at St Elbo's Schol for Gels . . .

Why has Mr Grant Aid, the popular social studies teacher been removed from the staff? Why are there six periods of Domestic Science each day? And why are *all* the algebra solutions UB40?

Find out the answers to these problems and the meaning of the sinister Compulsory Unemployment Training Scheme in 'The Four Marys Against the C.U.T.S.'

Advert for show by Little Women

'MORE' depicts women trying to survive the pain of asking and facing questions about the 'hidden disabilities' of their lives, anorexia and agoraphobia. In a world of old rope and broken glass, they ask: 'What does it cost you to say "I'm alright" and what does it cost me to listen to that lie?'

Gay Sweatshop

The romantic fantasies of many Japanese girls focus on love affairs with dashingly handsome women dressed as men. These *otokoyaku* ('male roles') are the stars of the 400 member Takarazuka Grand Theatre, the female counterpart of the all-male kabuki theatre. They have borrowed heavily from English to describe themselves positively because the Japanese word for 'homosexual' connotes psychological disturbance. (It is *doseiai,* literally 'same-sex love'.) The women who prefer to call themselves *rezubian* discuss whether to *komu auto suru,* just like English speakers talking about 'coming out' of the closet. The English insult 'lezzie' even has the Japanese equivalent *rezu.*

Cherry Kittredge, Feminist Forum, Japan

Girls Jumping Rope

In this play the child rehearses the part he wishes or she wishes to assume in adult life. The girl jumping rope acts out the to-and-from movement of the man during sex intercourse. Her own body takes the part of the active man, while the swinging rope imitates her own body adjusting to the movement of man's. In this game, girl acts both the role of man and of the woman. Thus the girls go through unconscious preparation for their future sexual function as women.

Marion Sonneberg, Journal of Irreproducible Results

Pornography is an act of violence against women, argues Ms Daniels in this provocative and bold drama; but she argues with wit and humour. A prostitute extols the joys of teenage contraception; a female social worker throws under a train a man who propositions her.

Cardiff Sherman, THEATRE TIMES

fashion

Nikki Craft said that bathing suit tops "simulate bondage" and that forcing women to wear them called attention to women and had caused men to consider breasts as sexually stimulating. "Women must refuse to collaborate in their victimization by silence," she said in an interview, "and we cannot tolerate images of ourselves being bound and tortured for men's profit and sexual gratification. I am pro-nudity and sexuality and against exploitation and sexual objectification for profit."

NEW YORK TIMES

food and drink

The pros and cons of vegetarianism came up again and again. "Eating cut up dead animals is bad for you, like heterosexuality," said one woman, maintaining that once you realise this it is easy to give up both. Another woman agreed that meat and men were probably bad for women, but "I want my right not to be perfect."

BOOK NEWS, Harvester Press

For more than five years, successive managers at The New White Bear Berni Inn, Tingley, near Leeds, have offered a ploughperson's lunch, instead of the traditional ploughman's.

"The management changed the name from man to person when the Equal Opportunities Act came in, as they thought it would be wrong to advertise a ploughman's lunch, when the law forbids them to advertise for a barman or maid."

YORKSHIRE EVENING POST

Graffiti, King's College, London

THE SCOTSMAN

SISTERBITE – 190 Upper Street, N1

This is a vegetarian cafe upstairs from 'SISTERWRITE'. (Men are not allowed.)

We hope you can find time to eat in this women's collective cafe instead of some male-dominated establishment. The food is good and not expensive. (Potatoes in their jackets are great!)

Cafe is non-smoking.

(No lift. Steep stairs, disabled women have been assisted to cafe. Loo on same floor as Sisterbite.)
Tues-Fri 12-5.30; Sat 11-5.30.

Kate Seal, Lesbian-Feminist Weekend Guide to London

NEW YEAR'S DAY
Fill the Air With Womyn!!

Start the year by showing the world that womyn are rising up and will be seen and heard!! Womyn all over the world are being asked to celebrate the dawning of the new year and the beginning of its first day by sending paper womyn into the air with balloons.

Write messages of goodwill, hope, and peace. Send them from your garden, or from high hills, from the top of a block of flats or climb a tree!

You can't keep a good womyn down!!!

With the element of air create a change in the element metal. As we send our positive energy into the skies visualise the heavy rigid cold fences becoming lighter softer warmer. Effect the metal vibration.

EXPECT A MIRACLE!!

Womynkind use our minds to melt away the barriers. (Please copy and give to other womyn.)

Greenham Womyn

Graffiti, Oxford wall

Arrests in 'Peace' Demo

EIGHT women from the "peace camp" at Greenham Common, Berks, appeared in court yesterday afternoon . . . The eight are: Sarah Hipperson, 55, Jacqueline Golding, 18, Charlotte Kaye, 18, Judy Van Dijk, 22, Trigger Graham, 18, Freda People, 26, Sue Hornagold, 18 and Elexei Earth, 18.

THE TIMES

higher education

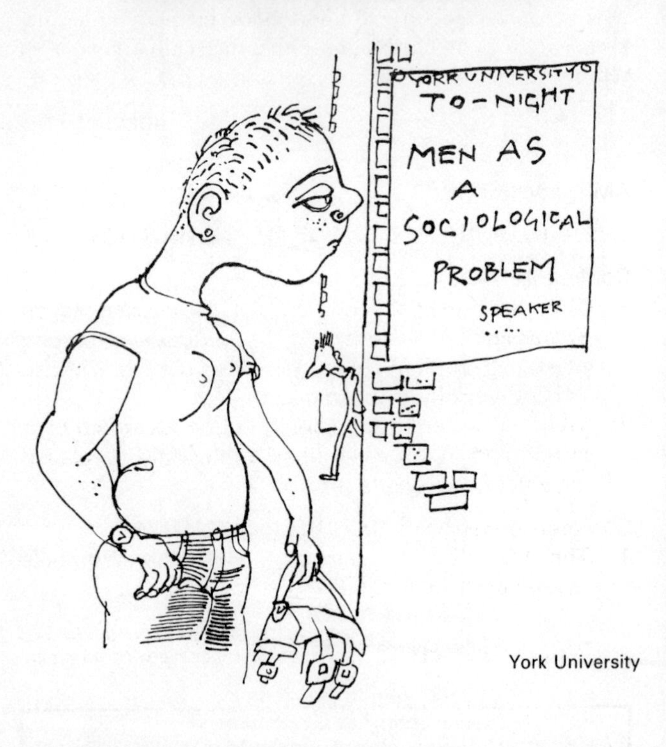

York University

The walls and doors of the women's toilets at the University of Sussex library were, and are, covered with women's writing. From this lowest seat of learning a polylogic testament to women's entry into discourse can be read in the round . . . that loo wall remains with me as an important event in the history of feminism, a moment whose appearance and significance we must work to understand.

Cora Kaplan, 'Formations of Pleasure'

But Lahey, who teaches at the University of Windsor, told a conference workshop that single women and lesbians now are forced to turn to unorthodox methods of getting pregnant to fight back against the "masculine control of reproduction."

TORONTO STAR

AMENDMENT 16

Tabled by: **WARLEY COLLEGE OF TECHNOLOGY**

Conference believes:

1. That wearing white should not be classed as an expression of virtue during the marriage ceremony and that women have the freedom to choose whichever colour appeals to them.
2. That the wedding ring should not be identified by a specific position on the hand and should be placed anywhere one wants it to be.

Conference instructs: **NATIONAL EXECUTIVE**

1. The Executive to campaign with the Women's movement to change these sexist attitudes.

National Union of Students Conference
held at Warwick University

TALKING POINT

The breast itself can be seen as a metaphor for our struggles

Trinity College Union newsletter

humour

Q: How do you get 16 elephants into a mini-car?
A: Simple – you seat 8 in the front and 8 in the back!
Q: How do you get 16 giraffes in?
A: You can't . . . it's full of elephants!
Q: How do you get 16 men in?
A: Ask the elephants to get out quietly. Inject each man with a tranquillizing dart. Bind ankles and wrists with strong twine. Remove seats, engine and shopping from vehicle. Whilst wearing sterilized gloves heave bodies in, using sledge-hammer to ram into place. Use plenty of woman power to lean on doors, bonnet and boot, to close. Lock up. Leave 12 hours (have a party) for drug to wear off, then all (elephants and giraffes included) stand around jeering and laughing!!!

Manchester Women's Liberation Newsletter

WOMEN DRAW

Published by the Women's Press. Price £2.95.

It is a fine collection of cartoons expressing humour on feminism, lesbianism and women's lives in general. In a nutshell, it is about life. It will, perhaps, provide material for Auberon Waugh and certain others in a well known right-wing rag.

John Payne, GAY LIFE – London's Alternative Magazine

in the courts

Radical feminist Andrea Dworkin is suing Hustler magazine for 150 million dollars for portraying her in cartoons as a lesbian. On June 28th, at a Lesbian Pride Week rally in New York's Central Park Dworkin told a cheering crowd, "being a lesbian means to me that there is an erotic passion and intimacy which comes of taste and touch, a wild, salty tenderness, a wet sweet sweat, our breasts, our mouths, our bleeps, our intertangled hairs, our hands".

Anderson Valley Advertiser

Four girls aged 16 to 18 turned to mugging because "all the boys at college did it and they thought why not the girls", it was stated at Inner London Crown Court yesterday. They hatched the plot during a typing lesson.

DAILY TELEGRAPH

letters to the editor

In Polly Toynbee's informative article I noticed that every case of demonic possession involved a woman. Could it be that in a world where most of the evil is perpetrated by men the male-dominated clergy find some measure of expiation in heaping guilt upon an apparently willing or gullible scapegoat?

The sins of the fathers will be visited upon the daughters! Not me mate.

Sincerely
Joan Byrne,
Benfleet, Essex

THE GUARDIAN

Graffiti, London wall

Dear *Spare Rib*,

In your report on the Greenham Common protest (SR 127) on 12 and 13 December none of the women mentioned the MEN, who, in their hundreds, turned up on the Sunday to the *women's* action. I was disgusted that these men could be arrogant enough to think that they were involved except in a purely menial capacity.

SPARE RIB

We would like to draw your attention to the fact that the Welsh Language is hostile to sexual equality. As Welsh speakers, should we not be ashamed of the fact that feminine words are forced to mutate after the indefinite article, while Masculine words are left alone? It is no wonder that Welsh men are so reactionary when their behaviour is rooted in the words used over a period of centuries. This is an integral part of the diseased thinking of men in every nation. Is it not high time that this linguistic slur on women was eliminated?

Translation of letter titled
'Gelyniaethus i ferched' in magazine 'Y Faver'

We have made a *little* progress, though. There was "Ms.", no longer subverted by its appendicular role to "Mr." There was the revelation by T. Grace Atkinson that our sisters could survive without the so-called "men" of our species – we need nothing from them but their sperm until we perfect a method of propagating through parthenogenesis or even fertilizing one sister's egg with the genetic material of another.

Mary Ann Foster, letter to MONDAY magazine, Canada

Why is there only one tampon dispenser in the Union building? Also, why do Tampax in the Union shop cost so much?

We already have to cope with pre-menstrual tension, period pain, tiredness, mess and inconvenience, why should we put up with being grossly overcharged as well? Take the 'men' out of menstruation and give us back free periods.

In disgust.

Sarah Ledger & Helen Russo, letter in
Manchester University Students' Union Rag

We are two women, a biological mother and a non-biological parent, who are engaged in challenging the law regarding parental status. As the law now stands it is not possible for two members of the same sex to have equal parental rights. It seems as though it is high time for action to be taken, considering the increasing number of lesbian couples with children and the use of A.I.

Letter in SPARE RIB

I'm in a dilemma. Tell me please where I've gone wrong.

Although I am a Lesbian I have always taken a deep interest in the affairs of my child-bearing sisters and have devoted much of my adult life to the Pro-Abortion Lobby.

However, at the same time I am prominent in the campaign to stop the culling of seals and the coursing of hares. Am I schizophrenic?

Letter to SUNDAY WORLD

I don't know what the proportion is of women to men contestants in Mastermind nor how the competitors for each session are chosen. But it does seem a pity that sometimes there are three women and one man. This means that if the man wins three women are eliminated at a stroke.

W. HAYWARD, letter to DAILY MAIL

The "Christmas" obscenities themselves show just how this evil chauvinism is institutionalised in our social structures.

Firstly, Father Christmas is a blatant male-chauvinist symbol. With his "facial hair" and "trousers", he stands for the exclusive male "breadwinner" bringing goodies to the bourgeois nuclear family. Superman Santa – who is never "black" – should be abolished totally.

Secondly, Christmas as a religious festival is itself thoroughly offensive in a multicultural society. A minority of Christians impose their silly superstitions, which even their own bishops do not believe, on everyone else, especially children.

The sooner we realise that a truly anti-racist and anti-sexist society demands the complete removal from schools and public life of everything to do with Christmas, the better.

Elaine Asghar, letter to FREE WALTHAMSTOW

listen with mother

ONCE UPON A TIME, when the earth was not so green and fruitful as it is now my daughter, strange creatures lived and ruled.

It was a bad time for us, then, my grandmother said, we were kept like pets. We had no names of our own and used to be called darling, my dear, old girl, and such names.

When the creatures called our people obeyed, for they demanded constant care. We had many menial tasks to do. Our backs were bent and we walked slowly with our eyes on the ground, not daring to look at our own kind. If we did, the creatures shouted at us (words like lesbian, and dyke were bad words then).

At that time we had no language of our own to answer them or even to talk to them, not that they listened. Sometimes we met secretly in Centres to discuss the vile and filthy habits of the creatures, habits such as spitting, shouting, pushing, beating, fighting, stealing from us and strutting.

The creatures had obvious genitalia and showed them whenever they opened their legs. Sometimes they handled them publicly. Perhaps this was the worst habit of all. All this time and for many years afterwards, and even now, our people tried to rid themselves of the creatures. In the centres I told you of, our people met and talked together, and our scientists worked and worked to disappear these creatures. But some argued against disappearing the creatures. That is a very sad and sorry story, o my daughter.

But now is the time for your short sleep. Tomorrow I will tell you how our people learned from each other, to disappear the creatures.

Then you will see why you must work so hard at your studies in genetics, and biology, and creativity.

No.

There are no more creatures now but I will leave a little light, in case you have bad dreams of them.

Short story, LYSISTRATA MAGAZINE

music

Workshops offered throughout the festival included:

**Womyn in Support of Central American Womyn's Struggles;
Lesbian Mothers & Lesbian Daughters;
Nutrition Information; Computer Networking;
Raised Poor & Raised Working-Class Womyn;
Lesbian Battering, Older Lesbians, and many others.**

Cinton led a tremendously successful workshop on comedy.

Michigan Womyn's Music Festival

HEATH

The band 'Ova' register a pitch of frustration and excitement with their song 'I Killed a Man In Self-Defence'.

SPARE RIB

WIGWAM BAM

One of the first feminist pop songs, telling the consciousness raising tale of how squaw Mini Ha Ha shed her culturally determined position of subservience and took on the dominant role of predator with the joyous yell

"Wigwam bam gonna make you my man!"

Eleanor Levy, RECORD MIRROR

Two women step forward, one wearing a painted cloak with collar and headdress of rainbow feathers, the other in shirt and jeans playing a guitar. She plays as the other woman sings the song of the rainbow dragon – how she's been asleep for the last few thousand years, and how the time's coming for her to wake at last.

With the music, the enslaved women stir. A good witch appears. To cheers from us watching, she and others bring wool out of their sleeves or pockets and start winding and weaving it round the startled patriarchs. Instruments are brought out, a drum, a pipe, and the music gets stronger and more rhythmic.

The women dance, encircling the patriarchs, winding them around and around firmly and gently with the wool until they are crouched powerless on the ground!

Liz Knight, London Labour Briefing

I also discovered other wonderful things like kirtan. Kirtan is a form of meditation, chanting mantra to music. Usually we chant in the ancient language of Sanskrit but sometimes in English. At first I was suspicious, wanting to know what I was chanting in case I was chanting to a male god.

MAGDALENE MAGAZINE

TALKING POINT

Although many may yearn for the lost elegance of the ballroom style, we should not forget that old-fashioned dancing only perpetuates old-fashioned values, trapping women in the roles that they have played too long.

Amanda Posey, THE GUARDIAN

occult

During the 15th, 16th and 17th centuries, the European witch-burnings took the lives of nine million women. These executions were preceded by an appalling catalogue of physical torture and sexual abuse. After the trials, many villages were left with only a handful of living women, the rest sacrificed to a perverted morality and twisted view of human behaviour.

The Theatre Centre, Ontario

FEMINIST NEW AGE TAROT

First of two workshops: Maddermarket, 75p

Historically, the use of tarot cards has always emphasised the division between men and women. Women have been viewed as passive and negative, virgin and whore. This reinforcement of the classical roles of women has arisen because of the continuing domination of patriarchal ideology in society and occult studies. What has been entirely forgotten is the true mystery behind the Tarot – that of the Androgyne/ Gynander within each and every one of us.

Norwich Women's
Book Festival Programme

Resurrect the ashes of
the women burnt as witches
resurrect the ashes
mould the cinders
stir the cauldron
resurrect those witches . . .

Resurrect
Resurrect
Resurrect

As for the boys playing
with their power toys
entoad them all.

Grace Nichols, 20th-Century Witch-chant

A plan for a "witch's garden" at Liverpool's International Garden Festival has stirred up a brew of protest for the organisers . . . The two women behind the controversial scheme have scoffed at the criticism. "Witchcraft played a major part in Britain's heritage, and the connection with mother nature is obvious," said Liz Brandon-Jones, one of the garden's designers. **"This is just another example of male domination over women."**

LIVERPOOL ECHO

POETRY CORNER

I had rather be a woman
Than an earwig
But there's not much in it sometimes.
We both crawl out of bed
But there the likeness ends.
Earwigs don't have to
Feed their children,
Feed the cat,
Feed the rabbits,
Feed the dishwasher.

Daphne Schiller,
'No Holds Barred', a book of women's poems

personal

Four lonely DYKE-SEPARATISTS-FEMINISTS from Japan (British/American) seek same in July/August. Hobbies include radical feminist politics, lesbianism, witchcraft etc. Box 714.

SPARE RIB

BLACK LESBIAN feminist student teacher and anti-sexist CHILD (4), on ICH waiting list, urgently need two rooms, ideally in women's house with another young child, but anything considered.

Advertisement – Islington Community Housing

WALKER – Brigid and Colin welcome another feminist (Leonie Harriet) a Sister for Ben and Chloe, born happily on September 16, 1984, at Bristol Maternity Hospital.

Ad in Personal Column of THE GUARDIAN

CLEIS. My name was chosen by me. It says a lot about who I am. Cleis is/was Sappho's daughter that makes clear my ancient connection to Wise/Healing Wimmin. I spent 15 years being a Midwife. The past five years have been about Midwifing for myself, supported by others, the Wise Woman/Healer/Therapist in myself. I see this unearthing as a never ending process.

SPRING LOOM, 5-Day Residential Reichian Therapy Group

AMERICAN LESBIAN wishes to meet pro-feminist gay man with view to friendship/marriage.

Ad in CITY LIMITS

MOTORCYCLE MECHANIC – Ref. WH 175/HG

Our Young Women's Motorcycle project is in need of a mechanic who is familiar with all aspects of small Japanese machines and can work in small groups operating from the base-line of a feminist perspective.

HACKNEY GAZETTE

GO-KART PROJECT – Ref. WH 180/CL

We are at present attempting to start a Young Women's Go-Kart Project and require a mechanic who is familiar with both training Karts (using Briggs and Stratton Power Packs) and racing Karts. This project is planned to operate from the base-line of a feminist perspective and we require someone committed to this mode of work.

CITY LIMITS

Society . . . preventing us from being strong and intelligent, beautiful in way we like . . . reclaim our potential for pleasure, strength and life. Reclaim our woman rhythms – *Kate would like to build a menstrual hut.*

Images of Women Newsletter

Lunar Cycles which opened in South London in September is Britain's first women only bicycle co-op. The impulse for a women's bicycle co-op came from frustration with mystifying bike repair manuals written by men and repeated experiences of being patronised and put down by men in bike repair shops . . .

OUTWRITE

WE ARE SIX WOMEN OFFERING OUR SKILLS:

Anne Dale is a teacher of yoga and women's studies and a counsellor. Carol Halliwell is trained in biodynamic therapy and massage. Daphne Lord is an artist specialising in masks and theatre crafts. Jane Malcomson is a trans-personal counsellor and astrologer who works with myth, the Tarot and nutrition. Alix Pirani is a bodymind therapist, psychodramatist and teacher of creative writing. Libby Worth performs and teaches dance and theatre.

Chesham Workshop Details

politics

FEMINISTS Demand Jail for 'Coercion'

Feminists on the women's committee of Labour-controlled Islington Council are calling for five-year jail sentences for men who employ "emotional coercion" in sexual relationships.

Under the committee's recommendations it will be an offence for any man to "force, threaten or coerce a woman, physically, psychologically or emotionally into sexual activity whether or not in the family and whether or not for profit."

DAILY TELEGRAPH

Feminist members of Birkenhead Labour Party have decided that during the season of goodwill men enjoy an unfair advantage through the "male stereotype" image of Santa Claus.

To correct the imbalance they have invented their own Mother Christmas who will make her debut tomorrow, dressed in blue and green, alongside a traditional Santa at a party for children of the unemployed and striking miners.

DAILY TELEGRAPH

The County Hall Lesbian Group has declared
Thursday March 1st

'Why Presume I'm Heterosexual' Day

CAPITAL GAY

A friend calls and says the looting after the recent disturbances in Handsworth, Birmingham, was carried out by middle-aged women. Not only did these women (should I call them housewives? should I describe them as black? It does matter) have the nerve to get their groceries in this opportune way. When Police Officers came along they hid their spoils and tut-tutted with the officers about the terrible lawlessness that surrounded them. I am amused and delighted: not because of the riots – because they will not solve Handsworth's problems – but because of the courage, humour, cunning and fortitude these women displayed. These are spiritual qualities, and – I realise it suddenly – they are what I think of as socialist feminism.

NEW INTERNATIONALIST

A cartoon character invented to alert children to the dangers of fire was condemned yesterday as sexist.

Feminists on the Labour-controlled South Yorkshire County Council are angry that publicity officers have chosen a friendly fire engine called Willie Water-tender to highlight the campaign.

Now a female version, Winnie Water-tender, is to be added following protests from County Councillor Pauline Gilbert.

DAILY TELEGRAPH

Women members of Sweden's ruling Socialist party yesterday called for the establishment of "erotic-free zones" in all work places. They said such zones would be like "no smoking areas" where men would not be allowed to regard women as sex objects.

THE TIMES

While the Committee on Safety of Medicines was debating whether to allow a new contraceptive jab to be available to the National Health Service, certain women's organizations, financed by the GLC, put out pamphlets that suggested that white doctors, backed by the police, would use this to "solve the immigrant problem" by rendering black females infertile.

DAILY EXPRESS

WE DO THINK THAT ALL FEMINISTS CAN AND SHOULD BE POLITICAL LESBIANS. OUR DEFINITION OF A POLITICAL LESBIAN IS A WOMAN-IDENTIFIED WOMAN WHO DOES NOT FUCK MEN. IT DOES NOT MEAN COMPULSORY SEXUAL ACTIVITY WITH WOMEN.

Leeds Revolutionary Feminist Group

TALKING POINT

Have anti-porn campaigners considered what effects greater censorship and forcing the sex industry underground would have on the working conditions of women in the sex industry?

Judith Kertesz
Women Against Rape, London NW6

As taxpayers, the Danes have long been accustomed to subsidising almost everything under the sun. Their education minister, for instance, now faces a parliamentary question about whether subsidised evening classes in lesbian massage are in keeping with the spirit of the adult education act (the letter is apparently not being contravened).

THE ECONOMIST

prison life

It is not surprising that Clare Carlton, imprisoned previously for the attempted murder of her first husband, had ruminated at length about the continuing domestic violence of Scottish men. "In Scotland men have all this aggressiveness . . ."

Pat Carlen, 'Women's Imprisonment'

Prisons may not exclude women from employment in jobs involving contact with male inmates, rules a US District Court in Michigan. It chides the state prisons department for 'stereotypical sexual characterisation' in concluding that it is more odious for a woman to view male inmates in the nude or performing toilet functions. The Court also says that inmates have no constitutional right of privacy that prohibits their being viewed by correctional officers of the opposite sex.

US News & World Report

protests

Radical feminists are urging all women to quit jobs, housework and even sex next Thursday.

They have backing from gay and lesbian groups, trade unions, workers co-operatives and black groups.

A leaflet promoting the protest calls on women to take whatever time off they can from office jobs, mothering, nursing, teaching, factory work and "sex work".

"Sex is work, emotional housework," said organiser Helen West, a 22-year-old unemployed Southampton woman.

"It's just another way we service the workforce."

SOUTHAMPTON GUARDIAN

Graffiti, Oxford Wall

S
N

College student sisters Jackie and Liz McCabe descended Manchester's 281ft town hall on ropes yesterday to mark International Women's Week. Jackie, 18, of Sandacre Road, Wythenshaw, said: "We considered it to be a phallic symbol and wanted to show that women could conquer it."

DAILY MIRROR

Saturday, January 21st, 1984, Holy Loch Base, Sandbank, near Dunoon, Scotland. 1pm – 6pm.

Many and varied opportunities to protest and survive. Blockade, Bonfires, Die-in, Anti-nuclear Scottish country dancing, Mural-painting, Cairn building . . .

Glasgow Women for Peace

Flying the flag in schools has been described as "phallus worship" and a "blatantly sexist ritual."

"Flag-flying is a blatantly sexist phallic ritual," spokesman for the Women's Action Group, Mrs Di Cleary, said.

"The symbolism of raising and lowering the flag once a day is quite obvious."

EVENING POST, Wellington NZ

WIMMIN'S ACTION DAY 9 AUGUST

A celebration of Wimmin's Action Day in conjunction with South African Wimmin's Day, to work on the connection between male violence, racism and militarism.
Contact Theresa McWomynus, as above.

SPARE RIB

13 Mon. Provincetown, MA – Womantide magazine is sponsoring a lesbian whalewatch.

Depart from McMillan Wharf at 10.30am for a 4–5 hour trip. Tickets at Womencrafts, 373 Commercial St. Info: (617) 487 9845.

Gay Community News

Oxford feminists, outraged that the city's bike lanes were adorned with male-bike-with-crossbar symbols protested, and won their point. Some of the new, painted signs now show female versions, without cross-bars. The *Oxford Mail* is suggesting that a future non-sexist answer might be to display family bikes with small wheels.

D. Catlow, THE GUARDIAN

Sticker seen near Greenham Common

religion

The term "clergy person" should be preferred to "clergyman", "God" should never be "he" and Jesus should be "he" as little as possible. Even the devil should be sexless according to a campaigning pamphlet published on Thursday . . . which declares war on sexist language in the church.

But Jesus Christ was male, "and we necessarily use some male nouns and pronouns when referring to Christ." Several of those "can certainly be reduced without approaching heresy", the pamphlet states. It is important not to emphasise his maleness, it says.

THE TIMES

Lectures on Mary, Mother of God, to be given at St James's Church Piccadilly, on Monday during Lent, explore experiences of women in the light of Christian tradition.

Among the subjects for discussion are

Mary and Liberation Theology
Mary and the Catholic Tradition
Mary and the Woman's Movement
'The Walking Madonna'

Mayfair, Soho & West End Advertiser

The cult of virgin motherhood is linked with morally repellent attitudes to sex and, even more, to women.

Rev. Don Cupitt, THE LISTENER

The reason women are more attracted to church-going than men may well be that they are more attracted to the idea of Jesus Christ than men, especially if he is taken to symbolise maleness broken and victimised, reduced to powerlessness.

Clifford Longley, THE TIMES

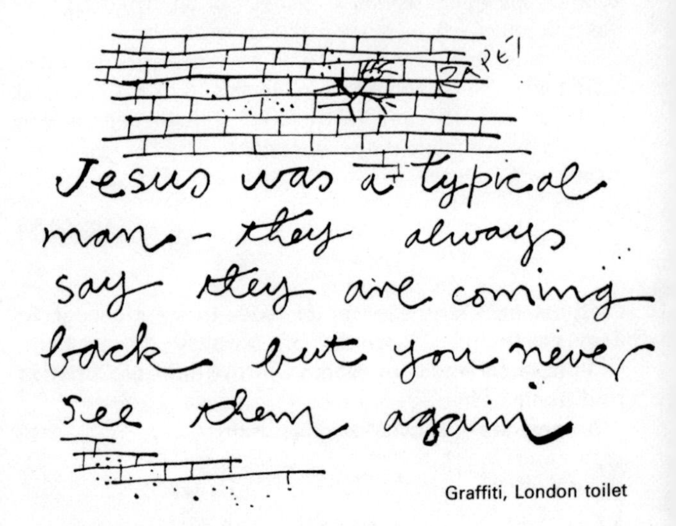

Graffiti, London toilet

BOOK OF GENESIS

In The Dinner Party Judy Chicago rewrote history, now, with The Birth Project, she has taken on the creation of the universe.

"That image of God reaching down to Adam . . . I just knew it wasn't true," Chicago told a Toronto audience last week. She proposes a new creation myth in which the cosmos comes from the "primeval vagina."

TORONTO STAR

Since taking on this assignment I have tried using the word 'goddess' instead of the word 'god' in all the customary ways. As an expletive: 'By Goddess' – 'Goddess damn it!' 'Thank Goddess', 'Goddess is in her heaven, all's right with the world.' And lots of other ways.

Rev. Mary Cleary in
Unitarian Universalist World

God our Mother, you give birth to all life, and love us to the uttermost. Your love surrounds us and feeds us. Within your love we find our home, our joy, our freedom. You open the world to us, and give us room to change and grow. As you love us, so you love all your children. Help us, dear Mother God, to catch something of your love: your delight in others' uniqueness, your care for their wellbeing, your grief at their suffering, your patience and forgiveness, your energy and hope. We thank you, we praise you, we love you: Through Jesus Christ Our Lord. AMEN*

* Many now feel that to ascribe only masculinity to God is inadequate. This prayer is offered for their use.

Christian Aid Handout

"I think God was making a feminist and political statement when he made man and woman."

Dean of Cathedral of St John the Divine, New York,
on the installation of the statue "Christa",
which depicts a woman on the cross, by Edwina Sandys

John 17:1-11 Jesus prays for the disciples

Having spoken these words, Jesus looked up to heaven and said, "*God my Mother and* Father, the hour has come; glorify your Child that your Child may glorify you, since you have given that Child power over all flesh, to give eternal life to all whom you have given your Child."

New Translation, NEW YORK TIMES

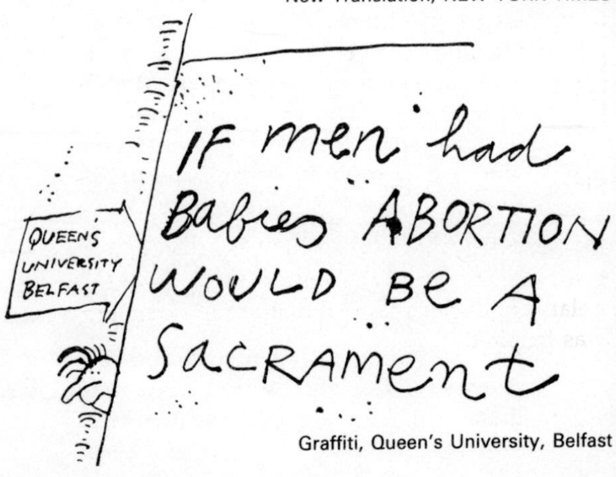

Graffiti, Queen's University, Belfast

In a pamphlet on menstrual taboos, Jo Nesbitt has suggested that the crucifixion is the ultimate image of male womb-envy.

"It is no accident that Mary is portrayed as giving birth in tranquillity or ecstasy as a reward for her asexuality, while her son takes on the suffering and dramatic role of the mother. The figure displayed on the crucifix is a male parody of the female experience of menstrual bleeding and childbirth."

Jealous of women's power to give birth, the male god must control the life of the spirit – which then takes precedence over mortal life and death.

Review of Pamphlet

NEWSFLASH

Canada's Anglican Church in Toronto yesterday suspended two deaconesses, one of them pregnant, after they declared their lesbian relationship and desire to raise a child.

IRISH TIMES

Since when has the Church *not* held 'morally repellent attitudes to sex and to women'? The Almighty is praised for not having 'abhor[red] the Virgin's womb'. As semen bears carcinogenic elements, Mary's avoidance of the 'relatively unclean normal method of becoming a mother' was inspired.

Letter to THE LISTENER

sayings of the weaker sex

The first human being a girl meets when she enters this world is a man: the obstetrician. As if she already understands that "Baby, it's a Man's World", she greets this advance man from the male establishment with an appropriately symbolic gesture. She pees on him. So far, so good.

Marion Meade, 'Bitching'

Men must recognise patriarchy for what it is, as the incarnation of rape, genocide, and war, of ecocide and necrophilia, and flee from it for their lives.

Rosemary Radford Reuther, The National Catholic Register

Coitus is punishment, I say. I am a feminist, not the fun kind. Coitus is the punishment for cowardice, for the fear of being alone.

Andrea Dworkin, 'Ice and Fire'

Every decision that a woman makes is right.

Germaine Greer, Danish TV Interview

sex

Men need variety in sex. If they don't get it from a partner they'll look elsewhere – in many cases just to prove their virility. Their basic insecurity again stems from the womb, which is hardly surprising when you consider that the male foetus is little more than a deformed female.

Pauline Cronin in THE SUNDAY WORLD

What do I need a man for? To give me support in a sexist world and thus to perpetuate my dependence for ever?

Sex with a man is a very political act. Every time I give in, take second best, every time I'm not totally honest to the point of, in my terms, unkindness, I'm giving in to the opposition.

SPARE RIB

sport

In spite of all that masculine bluster about men being strong and women being weak, men are really fearful that the opposite is true; they seek out ways to escape women and to band together with other men. Cricket legitimises the demarcation by men of yet another time and space where they can be free of women and united with other men.

Joan Smith, NEW STATESMAN

THIS SPORTING LIFE

The encouragement of women's further participation in an already degrading misuse of energy – sport (City Limits 110) – contains serious political implications.

This channelling of women's newly-found energy into harmless release, instead of fighting a perniciously brutal political system will benefit no one except politicians seeking to safely contain anger and frustration – and professional leisure entrepreneurs.

Susan Lovers, letter to CITY LIMITS

tips for men

How Men Can Act Innocent . . .

CODES OF CONDUCT FOR NON-SEXIST MEN

- Do not greet or accost or approach a woman. Even if you know her, be careful how you approach her. If she wants your attention she can always greet you.

- Do not colonise the whole pavement, whether alone or with other men. Ensure that there is enough space for others to pass without being forced onto the road or squashed against a wall or hedge.

- Do not hang around either on your own or with others, particularly in ill-lit places.

- Don't stand too close behind women in bus queues, etc.

- Rather change a carriage than let a woman be alone with you in a train, or tube. Those that don't will be prime suspects.

- Don't open conversations with women in public places. If a woman wants your attention she can address you.

- If you offer assistance to the disabled or mothers with prams etc, let the woman decide how you may help – do not just grab hold of a woman or child.

- Do not go out unaccompanied by a woman, unless it is absolutely essential, particularly after dark.

Birmingham University Guild of Students

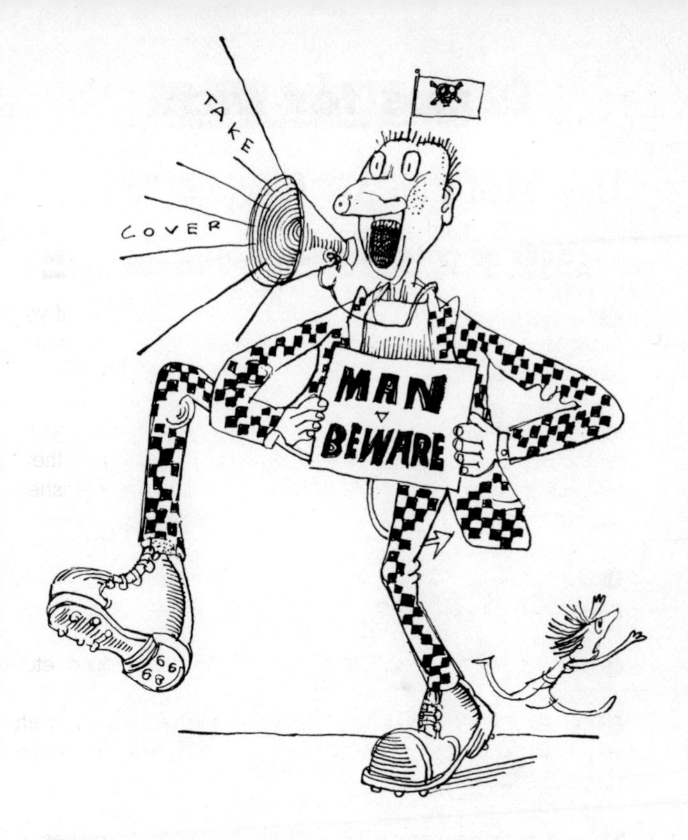

● Wear bright clothing so you can be easily seen – do not creep around in silent footwear.

Non-Sexist Code for Men, Leeds Other Paper

● If driving behind a woman in a car late at night, avoid following her any distance, slow down, overtake or change route.

Leaflet: 'Men in Public Places', Warwick University

toys and games

The alternative happy families pack is a light pleasantly designed game which aims to counter the usual sexist stereotyping in children's games. There's Carole the councillor, Poppy the peace campaigner and Gary the Gay all matching up in a family that isn't the normal heterosexual nuclear version.

Loretta Loach, SPARE RIB

A two-women company called 'Magination has developed a women's non-violent video game – Base Invaders! They got the idea from going to Greenham for a big action. Already involved in educational videos, they decided this game would be a great way of helping those who normally avoid computers to use and enjoy them.

Their promotional leaflet says "it can be played by men" – or at least, if you're not already a woman, you have to put yourself in a woman's place to play it. The game involves trying to cut down the airbase's fence.

SPARE RIB

Creatrix Catalog – Woman Rooted Crafts, Art, Music.

"Celebration of the Clitoris" Dolls

The idea for this doll came out of a self-help group I was part of. We realized that girl-children were beginning to hear about their vaginas, but not their clitorises . . . and thus continuing to learn about their sexuality primarily in terms of their reproductive capacities.

The dolls are 16 inches and have girl bodies of about ten years old. The shape of waist and hips is female. The arms and legs look strong and able. I like to think of them as studying some form of martial art and being really together physically.

The beads representing the clitorises are chosen with how the clitoris feels in mind, rather than how it looks. There are many different beads used.

I have a lot of fun making them because I make each one differently. By the time each one is finished, she has usually acquired a name.

The fabric is muslin, available in purple, brown, white.

Please designate colour preference. All dolls are $18.

CREATRIX CATALOG

wimmin's rites

This Rosh Hashana I celebrated with a group of eight women – five loving thoughtful Jewish women and three loving thoughtful non-Jewish women. We read and sang outdoors, under an arbour of oak trees and danced until midnight the dances our mothers have danced with each other for three millennia. We blew the shofar and listened to its haunting melody fade into the soft darkness.

Jane Litman,
Lilith, Jewish Women's magazine

That night four of us slept under the sky on Silbury, the pregnant womb of the Earth. Unthinkable to put up tents here . . . one doesn't put pegs in one's mother's belly. As a result a cold and windy night . . . but at one point both I and Jill felt a Fairy presence watching over us. In the early morning we went to say hello to Swallowhead, the vaginal opening in the white chalk bank which is the source of the sacred river Kennet, whose name originally meant "cunt". There we meditated . . . and then we went up the fields to the Mother of Death and Winter within the Earth of the West Kennet Long Barrow burial ground.

Monica Sjoo, Green Line

A further confirmation of the relationship of the Sun symbol to the source of human life was revealed to me when I attended a feminist class on the female body. By arranging a plastic speculum, mirror, and flashlight, I was able to see my own cervix (the mouth of the womb). It resembled a bright red doughnut, and the shape was exactly like the symbol for the Sun!

Donna Cunningham,
"An Astrological Guide to Self-Awareness"

We are mindful of the lunar calendar and mark all full moons and most new moons in some way. The Sabbats (Halloween, Winter Solstice, Imbolc or Candlemas, Persephone or Spring Equinox, Beltane, Summer Solstice, Lammas, Autumn Equinox or Festival of Demeter) are always celebrated by the womyn most keenly aware of magic, often with a visit to Silbury Hill, West Kennet long barrow and Swallowhead spring. Festivals and moons are sometimes marked by a group going widdershins round the base with candles and incense and doing something at each gate – singing, smearing the gates with menstrual blood, burning rune candles, etc. Some womyn wear ritual cloaks on these occasions and paint their faces at these times, as well as on days of mass actions like October 29, or for particular court cases. Altering our appearance in these ways strengthens our mental focus by separating those times from others, and such a visible statement of intent helps to spread the magic to other womyn. Hecate's circle is in the clearing at the main gate (yellow camp) and the sanctuary, a low lying piece of land not owned by the government, is a circle at the green camp. The blue camp, too, is creating a centring space in the woods. So far, these foci of rejuvenation have been protected and honoured by all creatures.

'Magic at Greenham', PANAKAEIA MAGAZINE

5.00-7.00pm. Feminist Spirituality: The Goddess Returns

Cindee Grace and members of the "Changing Woman" feminist spirituality group will use international slides, original music, and spontaneous ritual to take us on a mystical journey through time, exploring moon mythologies and goddess religions.

International Women's Week Programme,
University of Colorado

To me, feminism means the rebirth of the Goddess . . . she who is our infinite Self. For this to happen we must also act politically to throw off the shackles of capitalist and imperialist patriarchy . . . so as to free ourselves and to set free again our Mother, the Earth.

We are slowly beginning to regain some of our ancient menstrual, psychic, bisexual, visionary collective Woman-powers. It is slowly beginning to hum within us . . . deep, deep within . . . slowly, slowly we are reawakening . . .

Monica Sjoo, "Candlemas in Cymru"

words

The author of *Native Tongue*, published by DAW books, Suzette Haden Elgin has a professional interest in language. Currently director of the Ozark Center for Language Studies in Huntsville, Arkansas, Elgin has created 'Laadan', a language "invented by a woman for women, to express the perceptions of women", as background for *Native Tongue*. Elgin has been a frequent Guest of Honor at Wiscon, the Madison, Wisconsin, SF convention centered on feminist SF. Now, the Madison fangroup has published *A First Dictionary and Grammar of Laadan*.

Science Fiction Chronicle

In the pursuit of linguistic integrity and sexual equality, Ms Clare Short, 37, refused to make a so-called "maiden" speech. It was, she insisted, her "first".

SUNDAY TELEGRAPH MAGAZINE

Take for example 'Sweetheart', an examination of food metaphors as terms of endearment. Honey, sweetiepie, sugarplum, apple of my eye – all innocent enough, surely? Well . . . 'Do we detect a note of cannibalism here?' Coward asks, and goes on to suggest that in the predominantly 'masculine/material' use of such language (male lovers to their partners/women to children) we find a meshing of nourishment and sexual gratification in which 'there is a measure of sadism lurking beneath the surface . . . a language of devouring, gobbling up . . .' And in the sugar-based endearments through which women in particular are designated as objects of desire she hears connotations of decadent possession, voluptuous eating, 'a sweet-toothed western sexuality' in which women are the icing on a libidinal cake.

NEW STATESMAN review of 'Female Desire – Women's Sexuality Today' by Rosalind Coward

Definitions taken at random from a Feminist Dictionary, a deadly serious American tome just published in this country.

Herstory: 'The human story as told by women about women.'

Hes: 'Replacement of the phrase "Her/His".'

Man: 'Adult male human being. Today an obsolete life form.'

Manic: 'Of or like a man.'

MAIL ON SUNDAY

for further reading

Everyday Matters

NEW SHORT STORIES BY WOMEN

ABOUT THE AUTHORS

Caeia March. I was born in 1946 and grew up in industrial South Yorkshire. I have lived in London since 1964, and I work part-time, teaching sociology and women's studies. I left my marriage in October 1980 when I came out as a lesbian-feminist. I decided to leave my two sons, aged nine and seven, with their father. I am learning to spin and weave as a way of reclaiming both the matriarchal past and my own Manx Gaelic heritage.

Sheba Feminist Publishers

IN SEARCH OF OUR MOTHERS' GARDENS: Womanist Prose

ALICE WALKER

Harcourt Brace Jovanovich

The author's concerns are women like the characters in that story whom she defines as "womanish", serious, grown-up, in charge, as opposed to girlish, frivolous. The eloquent messages here come from Walker as a womanist, a black feminist.

PUBLISHERS WEEKLY

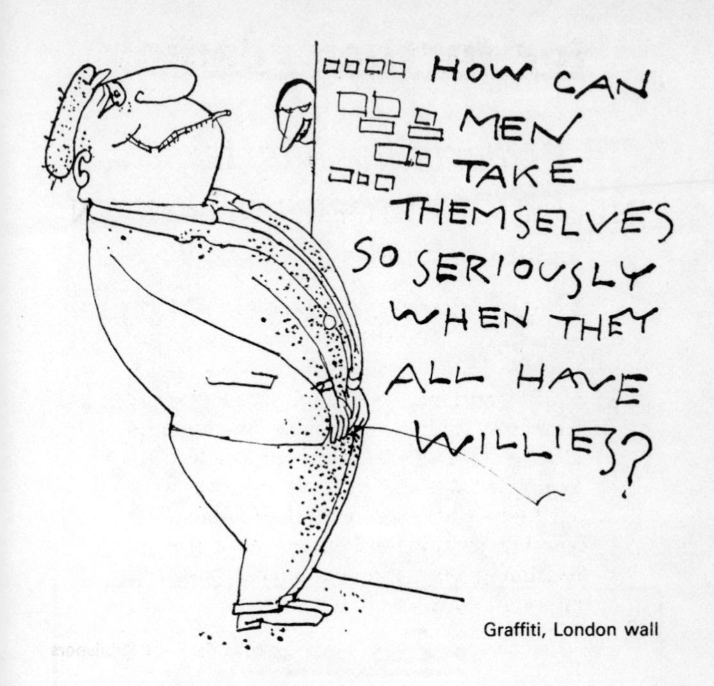

Graffiti, London wall

Prudie Finds Out
Natania & Litza Yansz

A cartoon comedy about the ecatcipation of an oppressed moggy.

My friend Daisy Mae Renn (2½) said 'I like the cats all doing things not just shopping' ('things' included Tai Chi and learning to bark in a cats' collective squat). Recommended present for all feminists aged 2½ up. (Routledge & Kegan Paul, £3.50)

Gair Rhydd, Cardiff University's Student Newspaper

Fairy Story Collective

RED RIDING HOOD 75p

An alternative version in which Red Riding Hood and her grandmother confront the wolf together.

Sisterwrite Catalogue

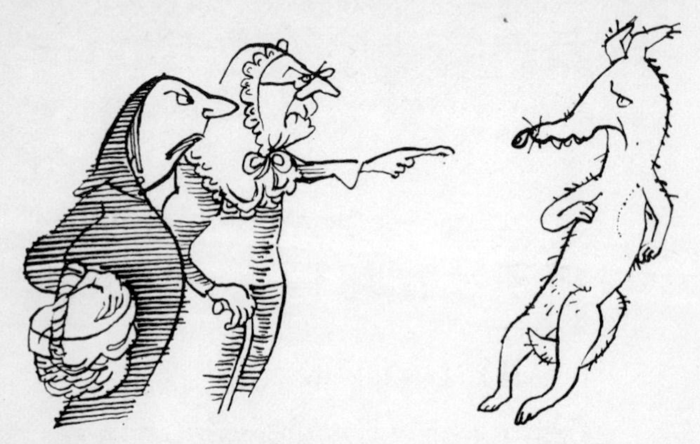

POETRY CORNER

sexism falls like quiet rain
constantly, softly seeping in
until we all become saturated
and it gently, ever so gently
so we hardly notice
does us terrible violence,
the ice forms, moulding us into
a shape uncannily uniform,
uncannily suitable for men.

Verse from 'For My "Apolitical" Sisters',
S/HE MAGAZINE

SELF INSEMINATION

Feminist Self Insemination Group, 198(2)? 47pp, £2.00

Pamphlet which is the work of a group of lesbian feminists, who met together to work out ways of getting pregnant through insemination by organising it themselves. They explain self-insemination as they arranged it and describe the difficult, and ambivalent feelings they had in doing self-insemination.

National Council for One-Parent Families Booklet

PURE LUST

Elemental Feminist Philosophy

MARY DALY

Daly has invented a modern feminist mythology. Its purpose is to help women liberate themselves from negative self-perception and anxieties about how men judge them. In this mythology Wantons, Nags, Fates, Dykes and Augurs courageously take personal steps to overcome patriarchy's hatred of women.

PUBLISHERS WEEKLY

WOOD & WATER

A Feminist Eco-Pagan Magazine containing articles on Wells, Forests, Nature etc.

Available from 4 High Tor Close, Babbacombe Road, Bromley, Kent. Single copies 85p, Annual sub. £3.40.

PANAKAEIA MAGAZINE

LESBIAN FEMINIST SCIENCE FICTION
A COLLECTION OF SHORT STORIES

The charm of green furry extra-terrestrials; the satisfaction of eerie revenge against a rapist; the ethics of survival in a world devoid of, and devastated by, men; the intricacies of a relationship between two women locked together in the isolation of space.

Only Women Press Catalogue

A THOUGHT

My pen is my penis
It relieves malaise in me
And much that issues from it
is bad news

Janet Webber, 33 Women Poets